Illustrated

By

Destin Andrews

of

Destoarts

ISBN:9798365510333

Forward

God sends treasure down to those who deserve it and sometimes to those who don't. The Bible says there are treasures stored up in Heaven for all who believe and trust in the Lord.

This book has been designed to reveal some treasure of knowledge that may help others believe. It is a project started in 1987. I recently began work on it again and have graciously completed it.

I hope its contribution will benefit all who read and believe in treasures from Heaven.

.

Acknowledgements

I would like to thank God for the talents he gave me and thanks to all my family and friends who believed in me. To my mother and father, Mary and Thomas, who taught me never to give up on my dreams. To my sister, Angela, who had the strength of ten Goliaths – rest in peace all.
Blessings to my older sister, Linda, and my baby brother, Thomas.

Much love to my two-year old grandson, Kaeden who is new to this world but holding firm to the dream and the legacy. And finally, to my daughter, Courtney – Dr. CBri - I thank you for the long hours and days of typing and helping me to finally get published – You are my light and my breath, the love of my life and truly a

blessing from Heaven.

33| Treasures from Heaven.

Table of Contents

A WILL TO LIVE

I cherished you dearly when you were born
The trumpeters signaled by four blows on the horn
You looked so small, so fragile and helpless
Everyone whispered how you had been blessed.

When they brought you to my room
I reached nervously for your small hand
I felt a cold gripping surge of gloom
As I held onto your tiny I.D. band.

You seemed to sigh as if relieved
To feel your mother's first soft touch.
It was then I knew that I believed
That I'd love you oh so very much.

Since that time we've been through a lot
And you've grown into such a beautiful tot.
No one could know of your struggle to live
If only they knew what you had to give.

Years have gone by since that time
You're now successfully in your prime
Forever proving that you persevered
Taking this world with no fear!

This poem is dedicated to my daughter, Courtney Briana
Geneva, who put the light back into my life with her will
to live.

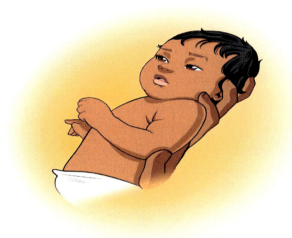

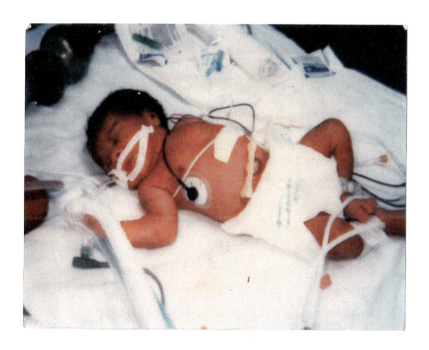

A Love Not Imagined by Even a Few

The love we share between us two
Is something no imagined by even a few
It's pure and simple and beautiful
Sent by God from Heaven, so dutiful.

No one could ever take your place
You've opened and brightened my empty little space
I pledge to make you happy as your wife
Together we'll be for rest of our life.

When I say those vows on our wedding day
A happy life with you I'll always pray
For nothing should separate us two
Not anything imagined by even a few.

Dedicated to you I'll always be
For you are the one who holds my key
You have opened my heart and finally my arms
With your beautiful ways and your wonderful charms.

Lonely were all my days before you
I now pledge to be fully faithful and true
I give you my heart and all of my soul
My dreams and my love, not a part but the whole.

You came to me just when I needed you the most
I'll honor and cherish you with a toast
To You, To Me, To our happiness you'll see
To a love strong enough to set us both
free!

For A Love Not Meant To Be

Years of fun and games and play
Never thought I'd reach this day
No sleep, just thoughts
Always feeling so lost.

Days filled with wondering, mulling and asking
Trying to hold out, just keep on masking
Wanted to hold you, to tell you my love
Words just flew away like a windswept dove.

Hoped you would know, you would see
All the hurt that was pent up in me
Needed you near to protect and to cherish
Only had my pillow when things seemed nightmarish.

Heart feels so empty and oh, so cold
After our love just broke up, all sold
Couldn't think of anything to do
Just wanted your love, just wanted you.

What the future holds I do not know
So sure am I that I don't want to go
A love so real, so alive, so true
It was a love that could only be for you.

My heart and my soul I'd gladly give
For just the chance that we may live!
Must throw away all the love that was felt
Because the cards had been so cruelly dealt.

MAN MADE LOVE

My world has changed so very much
I feel as if I've been tossed in space

I'm left all alone in a cold, eerie place
Where hardly can one find a good solid brace

I want to live and be a normal person
My work here is not even halfway done

Love had evaded me for quite some time
I'm holding on strong so I don't lose my mind

"Call on the Lord" is what everyone tells me
I pray constantly, but my way I can't see

I hope someone helps, someone shows that they care
This silence and loneliness are utter despair

I wanted to soar, to be free, just to roar
I can't even walk into the hall, out the door

I'm a prisoner inside and I don't know why
I gave it my best, a very good try

As I sit here quietly, waiting to be freed
I realize it all happened because of others greed

So, Harken! Dear people to hear my plea
You must never let anyone
Make you what they want you to be!

Live Like the Sun

The sun shines brightly on this day
It helps to guide men on their way
It warms the place where we abide
And beautifies the world outside.

Its rays can permeate the cold
To make all feel its warmth unfold
It makes the living things grow and live
With all the love it has to give.

These radiant rays always shine
To allow everyone to unwind
It illuminates into the dark
And starts with just a little spark.

A Soul That Lives!

Open my eyes that I may see

Open my ears that I may hear

Open my mind that I may think

Open my heart that I may love

Open my hands that I may give

Please Lord!

Open my soul that I may live!

Destiny

Once felt the steam of a heated world
Never knew who'd be the one to be hurled
Ran here, ran there, searching everywhere
Trying to avoid their thorny lair

    No love, just hate
    Was it just my fate?

Looking for my home, my place to be
Darkness surrounding, enveloping me
Tried to talk, to tell it all
Afraid I might stumble, break down and fall
Wanted to write all the things I had seen
How this world was crazy, so vicious, so mean.

    No love, just hate
    Was it just my fate?

Not many friends will be found
When they lay me under the mound
May there be peace, quiet, some tranquility
This world knows only change, no stability.

    No love, just hate
    Was it just my fate?

Too tired to fight, can't take no more
Done broke down and eaten at my inner core
Signs say slow down, signs say Stop!
Got to heed the call before I drop
This world is too cold, too cruel, too uncaring

wants to break me, make me lose my bearing.

     No love, just hate
     Was it just my fate?

No love, just hate
Is it just Man's fate?

To my family and to "All who make their own Destiny."

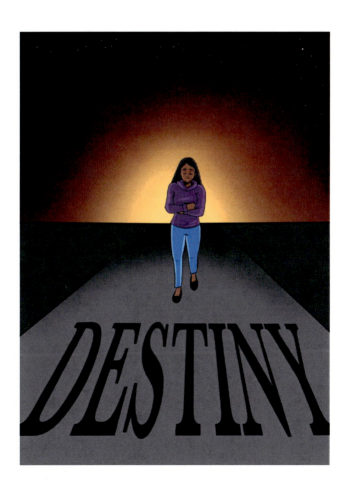

Pangs of a Smarted Heart

Loved you so, but you didn't know

Wanted your heart, though you walked out the door

Tried to call you, to tell you my love

Pushed me away, with your hot-headed steam

Darkened my way, when you dissolved our dream

Turned your head, and showed me your back

Opened the door, while you closed your heart

Denied our love, like a player who was smart.

A Prisoner of My 'Self'

Now I know why Maya Angelou wrote
    about the caged bird singing

As I sit here hurt with my eyes
    red and stinging

I reminiscence reluctantly about
    things in the past

Of friendships gone sour, how
    nothing ever lasts

I sit here lonely in my own
    little prison

I don't even care if the sun
    hasn't risen

My thoughts aren't my own
My life has all gone
I sit here as a caged bird
Who can never be heard

Because I can not use my voice
I doubt that I will ever rejoice
I sit here sad and all alone
Uttering not a word, just a moan.

Love Opens the Doors of Life

Beauty lies within the skies
A sun-drenched day so full of hope
Feather-soft clouds cause many tranquil sighs
Nothing to worry, no need to mope.

Charity can be found in all
Life holds riches for us to claim
We all must stand strong, lest we fall
So few to answer, so many to blame.

Love is a feeling we all possess
It's the soul of man that opens doors
Every human being is truly, truly blessed
With the light of the Savior, supremely yours!

STRIFE

I've felt the bonds of a distraught dream

Tasted the salt burning through my wounds

No more will I be placated, trampled in the dust

Trying to please a world so distraught and unjust.

Making a purpose for my strife

Waiting to hear a sign of life

Touched by The Master to go home

Winning the "Crown" after the storm

In the dust from whence man was created

There also burns the Fire (HELL)!

Mistaken Love

I met you first on a warm August morning
You smiled down on me as you sat in your big truck
I looked up from my car into your beaming face
I jumped out spilling coffee everywhere
Trying to get breathing space
I tried to approach you day after day
But I was scared you would reject me or try to play
I came to you finally to offer friendship
I was eager to know if you were a friend
I offered my hand and an excuse for a date
You called and I answered inviting you over
We met at my house on a warm October night
I was timid but eager to have you in my sight
When we kissed that night for the very first time
I knew that I wanted to be with you for the rest of my life
We made love until we were worn and tired
Blown away by our breaths, we were on fire
Oh how beautiful, a love so transparent
The world saw it first and made it apparent.

Two Hearts As One

Our hearts were two when we met a year ago
After we touched it was clear we both wanted more
I was so scared and alone before you came
Everything was turned around and nothing was the same
I remember you always for you have my heart
I knew I loved you from the very start
Together we'll be in holy matrimony
Our love is so real it's not a phony
When I walk down the aisle
I'll do so with style
Because you are the reason
For our beautiful love season
I come to you pure and ready
All this excitement has me so leady
Our hearts will beat as one
For the rest of our life
My love for you weighs over a ton
Because you'll be my husband and I'll be your wife.

A Pledge of True Love

Give me your heart and all of your love
Send me your kisses on the wings of a dove
Let me know that I'm wanted and needed
Make me your mate and you'll be well treated.

Now that I'm yours and yours alone
You must promise to make our love full grown
Together as one we can help each other
As long as we remember not to smother.

I love you, my friend, with all my heart
I pray to God we will never part
You vowed to love me for all my life
To make me happy as your wife.

Always true to you I will be
Your guide and your light to help you see
We will announce our love soon in a planned
ceremony
That will strengthen our bond in holy matrimony.

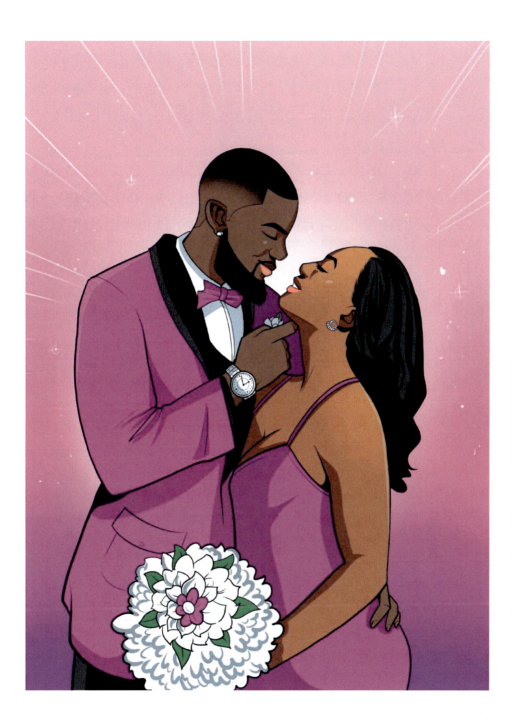

Purity in Today's World

The church steeple stretched high into the
sky
A symbolic cross perched proudly at the top
Made me feel warm and emit a soft sigh
To know that the miracles of the Master
never stop.

A guide to me He'll always be
Providing security and tranquility
Pushing me forward to conquer His world
A small fragile person turned into a
beautiful pearl.

Touched me with a jolt of love
Opened my mind to see the truth
Loved me so unconditionally
Remaining with me until the glorious end!

His Healing Ways

The things I've been through in my life
I'm glad to be alive and free of strife
I've come a long way and I've learned a lot
I'm grateful for happiness and all I've got.

My world is no longer a horrible place
I've finally found peace in my own little space
I'm making a way and I'm facing the world
I've opened my heart and found a gleaming white pearl.

Please listen, dear people, or all who might care
You've got Jesus to call on when Life's all you can bear
Just lay down your burdens and lift up your head
Look to the sky and follow His tread!

A Free Spirit – One Sign of Wellness

Doors slam shut loudly as if signaling a definite end

Patients walk around, each searching for a friend

All are restless with not much to do

Many show signs that escape is just for a few

Hoping to be let out soon

Waiting to sing out a happy tune

Want to be free to express and excel

Ready to move on with life and get well.

Dedicated to a "select" group of patients at
Memorial Hospital, Savannah, Georgia

God's Gift to a City at Christmastime

Riding down the highway, everything was all covered with ice.

The temperatures were below ten degrees, nothing was left unwrapped.

No birds or animals flounced around, all was soft and blistery quiet.

As we pulled into Savannah, Georgia, all eyes were set aglow.

For as far as we could see, there was nothing but white fluffy snow.

Never before had there been a time when it had snowed on Christmas Day.

Surely, it was a God sent miracle to tell us not to lose our way.

Perhaps, this was a day to remind us of what He had to pay.

Four Walls

All look the same. All colored the same.

None an original. None with a name.

Sat facing one wall

A wall of doubt, confusion and hatred

Listened to footsteps moving away, coming to

Heard paper that rattled, every movement

Every sound that vibrated

Made me cringe and recoil, made me scared and distorted

Ready to strike at anything in the air

Confused, frightened, of what...I don't know!

A Compass To Life

I look to the East
I look to the West
What beguiles me?
I can not guess.

Is it my dark chocolate skin
Or my curly black hair
The swell of my lips
Oh why do I care

I look to the East
I look to the West
What beguiles me
I can not guess

Is it my high held head
Or my strong sturdy stance
The surety of my voice
Oh now should I dance?

I look to the East
I look to the West
What beguiles me
I can not guess

Is it my rich ivory smile
Or my thick shapely legs
The fullness of my breast
That brings out my best

I look to the East
I look to the West
What beguiles me
I can not guess.

It's my beautiful black body
Or my smart, intelligent mind
It's the strength of my tone
Oh, yes I am one of a kind!

AWAKE, ALIVE, THANK GOD I SURVIVED

Climbed astride a height less mountain
All tired, weary and worn
Never knew a day of rest
Only push, since the day I was born

Swam beneath a bottomless sea
Nearly drowned, gasping and groping
Almost lost my sense of reserve
But lo, remembered the days I was hoping

Walked across a borderless land
Forever looking, lonely, blindly lurching
Always tried to find a haven
Barely reached, must continue searching

Flew up into a never-ending sky
No more worry, fear or pain
Finally reached my goal, my calling
Nothing to lose, so much to gain.

The Sky Reflects Heaven's Glory

In winter I saw a tree outside
Its branches bare, they looked so fragile
They seemed to touch the sky up high
As if to hook a roaming cloud.

The clouds roll by majestically
Their slow movement barely can we see
As they billow into weird and different shapes
They glide serenely across the open spans.

This openness stretches vast and wide
It seems a place of forever nothingness
But truly it reflects of infinite beauty
Of the days when some will face heavenly glory.

GOING HOME

Woke up happy and alert
Energy pumping up in spurts
Knew I'd make it happen soon
Once I sang my happy tune

Leaving this prison to return home
Anxious to see the golden dome
Freedom to soar and really stand tall
Release today means I will not fall

No more crying, no more pain
No more walking in the cold rain
I'm gonna make it, I've got to try
I'm gonna reach up and touch the sky!

INCARCERATION

Today I left the world outside
To enter a place where no one can hide
I stood behind a wall of glass
And watched the living things go past.

They locked me up inside this lonely place
Where everything slowed to a turtle-like pace
I wanted to scream, to just run away
But they kept me here, yes, they made me stay.

I don't know when they'll let me go free
This prison may soon, eventually kill me
Although I once welcomed tranquility and rest
I must move on to pass life's test.

I really want to live and soar
Grateful to them who unlock the door
Maybe soon I will stand tall
Straight and secure, I will not fall
Ready and waiting to answer His call.

Untitled

Lonely were all my days before you
I now pledge to be fully faithful and true
I give you my heart and all of my soul
My dreams and my love not a part but the whole

You came to me just when I needed you the most
I'll honor and cherish you with a toast
To you, To me, To our happiness you'll see
To a love strong enough to set us both free!

The "Crown" Belongs To All

He came from Heaven above
To spread God's message of Love
True to heart He shed His Blood
Gave man another chance
To restructure the Dance.

Be not mindful of scorn
Don't look outward for love
Find peace inside your heart
Search steadfast to the end
Lift up with strong legs, arms and hands
Reach out and claim the "Promised" Crown!

Glory to God in the Highest

Climbed astride a sprawling mountain
All tired, weary and worn
Never knew a day of rest
Only push, since the day I was born.

Swam beneath a bottomless sea
Nearly drowned, gasping, groping for air
Almost lost my sense of strength and reserve
But, lo, remembered the days when I was
fair and hoping.

Walked across a borderless land
Now defunct, decrepit, inane
Always tried to find my own space
Barely reached a haven sought.

Flew up into a never-ending sky
No more worry, fear or pain
Finally reached my goal, my calling
Oh, what Glory! Found a place to rest
before falling.

If You Here Today, You Better Pray

Babies born every minute in a day
Plenty folks worry about losing their way
Days shine somberly on a world filled with
tension
Nights bring dark hopes of long worked for
pensions

> Ain't got long now
> If you here today, you better pray

People sing songs that reflect His spirit
Nobody listens, they don't even hear it
Clocks tick furiously while church bells
chime
Everybody waits for His promised time

> Ain't got long now
> If you here today, you better pray

A Vow So Strong

Lonely were my days before you
I now pledge to be fully, faithful and true
I give you my heart and all of my soul
My dreams and my love
Not a part but the whole

I understand what our lives mean
It's clear to me this is destiny
Go fast, go slow keep up the flow
We're together now so let everyone know

You came to me just when I needed you
most
I'll honor and cherish you with a kiss and a
toast

To you! To Me! To our happiness we'll see
To a love strong enough to set us both
free!

I Was Once Somebody's Child
(A Child of God)

I was once somebody's child
But now I've got to rest my body
Rest my spirit
Rest my soul
Rest my mind lest I grow old.

My Father sent me to do His Work
He told me many would deny every word
Be careful not to believe what you heard
Hold on tight and let it be
Soon my child and you will see

Born to serve Him and only Him
Be a teacher, a leader just for them
Spread the Word - Remember Me
I will return and Comfort Thee!

The Day They Shut the Country Down

The day the virus hit the ground
We're all in this together they vowed

They suspended all activity
People scrounged to help each other

Isolation, Desperation, Polarization
They shut the country down

People dying from this COVID monster
It ravaged young and old

Hunker down – Don't leave your homes
Stay inside – Don't spread those germs

Scientist looking for a cure
When will it end, no one's for sure

God has a way of opening our eyes
Pray for His Mercy before anymore die.

A Prayer For A Puzzling New World

Heavenly Father,

As You watch over us here in this puzzling New World

Please protect and take care of us

For we, as Your children, encounter new experiences everyday

I pray that Your love will carry us through these days

And take us to a time where no man is a prisoner/ and no man is a fool

We who are worthy of your graciousness vow to honor Your Laws

Just as we are, O Lamb of God, we must follow You to the end.

Please Bless all family members and keep them strong to perform Your Will

Watch over and take care of the children for they are the innocent

Help us teach the true way of Life

For all our knowledge and strength come from You alone

Bless and Protect All who are believers of Your existence

Though we may fall short of Your Law through sin

Forgive us Father

I Pray These Things.

In the Name of The Father, who gives the Gift of Life!

In the Name of The Son, Jesus Christ, who died so that we may live!

And for the Holy Spirit, who is always with us to show us the way to a fruitful life

Please Father in Heaven

We ask these Things of You

Amen

Caricature of My Family
By
Destin Andrews, Illustrator

Author's Bio

In 1985, I came to the field of education as a paraprofessional of mentally handicapped students. Several teachers at the school where I worked were impressed with my engagement and encouraged me to become a teacher. I did so and have never looked back.

I acquired my certificate in Reading Language Arts and Social Studies. I also received a Master of Education and an Education Specialist in the area of Administration and Supervision. As part of my authorship, I am looking forward to publishing a series of children's books after Heaven's Treasure.

As a young child, I instinctively remember playing school with my neighborhood friends. The memories of writing on the chalkboard and using the thick white chalk and large dusty eraser are as vivid to me as if it were yesterday. I mimicked my teachers and corrected my students as if I were – a teacher. In my family, there was always a standard of behavior and authority for educators. They were seen as motivators and givers of knowledge.

When I became a teacher I became a motivator and a giver of knowledge. Teaching was a way that I could share my "gifts" with others. I wanted my teaching experience to "change the world" for my students.

Throughout my teaching years, I have come to realize the number of children I have influenced. Hundreds of students have been enmeshed in my heart. I have been instrumental in molding, motivating and changing the lives of every child I have encountered.

I realize too that one day I may recognize a familiar face as the President, the Governor or the Mayor. I may even see someone on satellite tv or walking on the moon. Each time pull into a Burger King, shop in Wal-Mart, go to a Wells Fargo, stop at the grocery store, visit a hospital or walk into a school, I am greeted by one of my students.

There is no other feeling that can replace that experience. It is as if you gave birth 100 times to each of those "little people." They are and will always be a part of you. And yet the strange thing is that they revel in seeing you when they are all grown-up. Just as proud as you are of them, they are as proud of you.

An old proverb written by an unknown author states: *Genius is undiscovered gold and talented is the teacher who struggles, finds, and helps all students develop it.*

As every school year unfolded, I must admit that I found gold in every child that entered my room. My only prayer is that each child would radiate and provide strength to reflect what they learned to help them make a positive effect on the world. As teachers, we have been given a great responsibility to train those who must grasp the future.

I hope I have molded and shaped each nugget into a fine filigree chain, gleaming proudly for the world to use and worthy to be worn by the loftiest king or the lowliest servant. One poem penned by an unknown author states:

Who am I?

Who Am I, to teach the children?
When there is so much I do not know.
How can I teach the importance of loving
When I struggle so?
May my students always see
That my teaching does not come from me.

Author Unknown

Made in United States
Orlando, FL
24 August 2023

36379614R00031